Why do horses wear shoes?

Jinny Johnson

Miles Kelly

First published in 2011 by Miles Kelly Publishing Ltd
Harding's Barn, Bardfield End Green, Thaxted,
Essex, CM6 3PX, UK

2 4 6 8 10 9 7 5 3

Publishing Director Belinda Gallagher
Creative Director Jo Cowan
Editorial Director Rosie McGuire
Editor Carly Blake
Editorial Assistant Lauren White
Volume Designer Sally Lace
Cover Designer Kayleigh Allen
Image Manager Liberty Newton
Indexer Gill Lee
Production Manager Elizabeth Collins
Reprographics Stephan Davis

ISBN 978-1-84810-459-4

Printed in China

British Library Cataloguing-in-Publication Data

A catalogue record for this book is
available from the British Library

ACKNOWLEDGEMENTS
The publishers would like to thank the following
artist who has contributed to this book:

Mike Foster (character cartoons)

All other artwork from the Miles Kelly Artwork Bank

The publishers would like to thank the following
sources for the use of their photographs:

Dreamstime.com 12 Fanfo
Fotolia.com 8(c) Jürgen Hust, (r) Bernd Meiseberg;
9(r) Linda Macpherson; 16(l) Tan Kian Khoon,
(rb) Sven Cramer **iStockphoto.com** 8(l) Leah-Anne
Thompson; 9(l) Claudia Steininger; 10 james boulette
Rex Features 28 Rex Features
Shutterstock.com 4-5 Eric Isselée; 7 Laura Gangi Pond;
16(rt) Kondrashov MIkhail Evgenevich; 15 mariait

All other photographs are from:
Corel, digitalSTOCK, ImageState, PhotoDisc

Every effort has been made to acknowledge the
source and copyright holder of each picture.
Miles Kelly Publishing apologises for any unintentional
errors or omissions.

Made with paper from a sustainable forest

www.mileskelly.net
info@mileskelly.net

www.factsforprojects.com

Contents

Are horses the same as ponies?

Horse

Horses and ponies are in the same animal group, but ponies are smaller. The height of a horse or pony is measured in 'hands'. To be considered a pony, a horse must be less than 14.2 hands (148 centimetres) tall at the withers (base of the neck).

Food on the move!

Since the 1800s, nosebags have been used to feed horses on the move. They are also useful for horses that are messy eaters!

Farmer

Shire horses pulling a plough

which horses worked on farms?

Shire horses were bred to pull heavy farm carts and ploughs before modern tractors and trucks were invented. They were used for this job because they are big, heavy and strong.

Pony

calculate
Try working out your own height in hands. There are 10 centimetres (4 inches) in a hand.

when were the first horse races?

People have probably raced horses since they first began taming them, over 5000 years ago. In ancient Greece, horse racing was part of the Olympic Games and the riders rode without saddles!

What are the points of a horse?

The points are the parts of a horse's body that you can see. Each point has a special name, such as withers, muzzle and fetlock. People who work with horses have to learn the names for all of the points.

count

How many socks and stockings can you find on the horses in this book?

Back

Dock

Hock

Fetlock

Hoof

Do horses have good eyesight?

Yes, they have excellent eyesight. They can see in almost every direction because their large eyes are on the sides of their head. This helps them to watch for predators (animals that hunt them).

Poll

Crest

Forelock

Withers

Muzzle

Magical horse!

A unicorn is a mythical horse with a horn on its head. Some people think the legend of unicorns came from the first sightings of rhinos!

Do horses and ponies wear socks?

No – but they have markings on their feet that are known as socks. A sock that goes up higher than the horse's knee is called a stocking. Horses can also have white marks on their faces, chests or heads.

Sock

Are horses and ponies colourful?

Yes they are! Horses and ponies have many different coat colours. Some of the colours and patterns have special names, such as bay (reddish-brown), chestnut (reddish-gold), dark bay (brown) and dun (sandy brown).

Chestnut
Reddish-gold

Skewbald
Patches of brown and white

Piebald
Patches of black and white

Palomino
Golden with white mane and tail

Why do horses wear shoes?

Horses wear metal horseshoes to protect their feet, or hooves. If horses run on hard surfaces without shoes, their hooves can get worn down. People who fit horseshoes onto horses are called farriers.

Farrier

Draw

Draw a picture of a horse and colour it in. Choose a pattern, such as piebald, for its body.

How can you tell a horse's age?

Vets can tell how old a horse is by looking in its mouth. A horse's front teeth change shape as it ages – from oval to round, and then to triangular. Older horses' teeth also stick out more.

Dark bay
Brown

Old Billy!

Horses usually live to about 30 years old. But Old Billy, an English horse born in the 1700s, lived to be 62!

Grey
White to grey

Do horses understand people?

Horses are clever animals and they can learn to understand commands such as 'walk' and 'whoa' (stop). Riders can also give horses instructions by nudging or patting them. Most horses are friendly, and they like to be talked to and touched.

Horse

Owner

High-speed horses!

Horses are fast runners, even when carrying a rider. The fastest racehorses can reach speeds of more than 60 kilometres an hour.

RUN

Run 100 metres as fast as you can! Ask an adult to time how long it takes you.

what do horses like to eat?

Horses and ponies eat mainly grass, or hay (dried grass). They often eat throughout the day. Horses and ponies enjoy other foods such as oats, barley and apples.

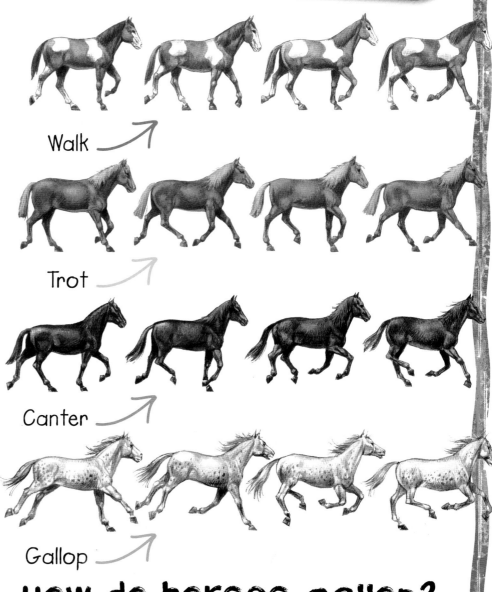

Walk

Trot

Canter

Gallop

HOW do horses gallop?

Horses can be trained to walk and run in four different ways – walk, trot, canter and gallop. When horses canter or gallop, there is a moment when all four feet are off the ground.

can horses swim well?

Yes, horses are very good swimmers. They float well in water and swim by moving their legs in a paddling motion. Horse trainers sometimes take their horses swimming because it's good exercise and helps to build up their muscles.

Swimming horse

Do some horses live in the wild?

Herds of wild horses live in many parts of the world. Most were originally tame horses that escaped from being kept by people. Only a few horses, such as the rare Przewalski's horse from Asia, are truly wild.

cave horses!

There are ancient cave paintings of horses in the Lascaux cave in France. They were created over 17,000 years ago.

which horse was as small as a sheep?

Mesohippus was a prehistoric, sheep-sized horse that roamed the Earth around 35 million years ago. Like other early horses, it was much smaller than most horses and ponies today. It was about 60 centimetres tall.

Mesohippus

Swim

The next time you go swimming, try to paddle the same way that a horse swims.

which horses live in swamps?

Groups of beautiful, white Camargue horses live in marshy swamps in France. They are small, but strong and sure-footed. Camargues are ridden by bull herders and can also be used for competitions and trekking.

Camargues

Find out

Look in books and on the Internet to learn about other animals that live in swamps.

when do foals start to walk?

A newborn horse, called a foal, can walk just a few hours after birth. Being able to move around and find food helps them to survive, and escape from predators.

Foal

Handsome horses!

Knights used to dress their horses up for tournaments (knightly contests) and battles. The horses wore coloured coats called trappers and helmets called shaffrons.

Do horses like to be on their own?

Most horses prefer company. In the wild, they naturally live in groups, or herds. Tame horses are usually happiest if they are kept in stables or fields with other horses.

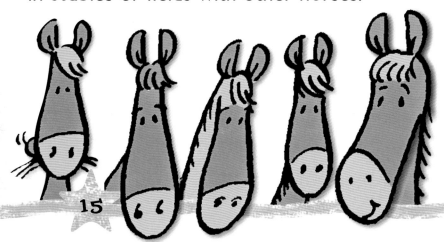

what is a hotblood?

Hotbloods are one of three types of horse. They came from the Middle East and Africa, and are often used in racing because they are fast. Coldblood horses are heavy, strong horses originally from colder areas in northern Europe. Warmbloods were bred by crossing hotbloods with coldbloods.

Warmblood

Hotblood

Coldblood

Why do horses wear plaits?

For shows and contests, a horse's owner may plait or decorate the long hair on its head and neck (mane). Plaiting helps the mane to stay neat as the horse moves around.

Plait
Try plaiting the mane of a toy horse to create some new horse 'hairstyles'.

Black Beauty!
Black Beauty is a novel written by Anna Sewell in 1877, about a black horse. In the book, the horse (Black Beauty) tells the story of his life and the people he met.

Horse being groomed

Do horses need grooming?

Yes, horses need to be groomed to stay clean and healthy. A horse should be brushed all over, and its hooves should be cleaned out. This removes bugs that could cause diseases and it makes the horse's coat look glossy.

How does a rider control a horse?

A rider controls a horse using reins – straps attached to a bridle around the horse's face. By pulling gently on the reins, the rider can tell the horse which way to go. Riders also do this by nudging the horse with their knees.

Bridle

Rein

Bit

Make
Using empty egg cartons and boxes, make a cart for a toy horse to pull.

Handy horses!

Ancient artworks show that humans have been using horses to pull carts and carriages for about 5000 years.

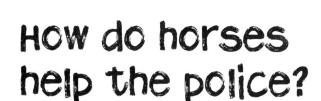

How do horses help the police?

The police use horses for transport in places where vehicles can't go, such as on a festival site or at a crowded street protest. Riding up high, police officers can get a good view.

Seat

Padding

Girth

What are saddles for?

Saddles help riders stay safe and comfortable. A saddle is a leather seat that is strapped onto a horse's back by the girth. A rider's feet sit in the metal loops, called stirrups, attached to the saddle.

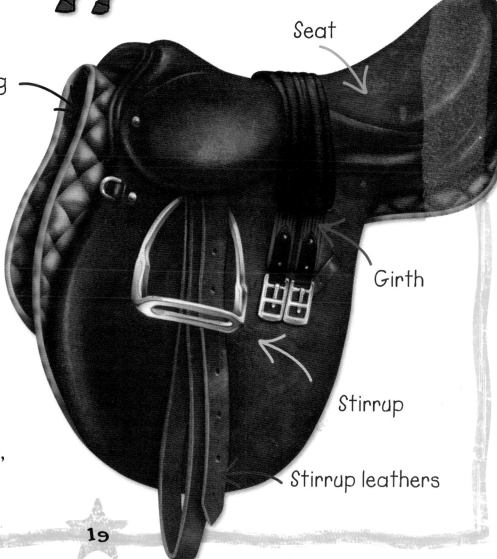

Stirrup

Stirrup leathers

Which pony is a champion jumper?

Rider

The Connemara pony, which first came from Ireland, is great at jumping. It can be ridden easily by adults and children. These ponies are often trained to take part in jumping and cross-country competitions, where horses have to jump over obstacles.

Jump
Set up some obstacles in your garden and see how high you can jump over them.

Did horses go to war?

Yes, horses have been ridden into battle since ancient times. They were trained to charge towards an enemy army without fear, and some wore special horse armour.

Warrior on horseback

Connemara pony

Horse of an emperor!

The Roman emperor Caligula was said to love his horse so much that he gave it its own house and servants!

What was chariot racing?

It was one of the most popular sports of the ancient Romans. In a race, horses pulled two-wheeled carts called chariots around a track called a 'circus'. There could be up to 12 chariots in each race.

Do horses have relatives?

Yes, they do. You can spot some of their relatives by their horse-like shape, such as zebras and donkeys. They belong to the same animal family as horses and ponies, called 'equids'. Horses are also cousins of rhinos and tapirs.

Zebras

BUCK UP!

Horses buck by lowering their heads and kicking up their hind feet. They developed this action as a defence against predators in the wild.

Shetland ponies

why are Shetland ponies so tough?

Shetland ponies come from the Shetland Islands, in the far north of Scotland, where it is often very cold and windy. They have developed short, stocky bodies and thick coats to keep warm.

HOW do horses talk to each other?

Horses use noises and touch to communicate. For example, 'whinnying' to call to each other, squealing or snorting to show alarm or excitement and nuzzling to greet and comfort each other.

Listen

When you go past a field of animals or visit a farm, listen out for the different animal sounds.

What does an angry horse look like?

If a horse or pony is angry or unhappy, it flattens its ears backwards against its head. It may also show the whites of its eyes by opening them wide. If you see a horse doing this, you should stay away in case it bites or kicks.

Ears are back

Think

Think about how you can tell when a person is angry or happy. How do they show it?

what makes horses and ponies ill?

Eating poisonous plants. Horses and ponies can't be sick, so if they eat something that's bad for them, they can't bring it back up. Foxgloves, acorns, laburnum and ragwort are some of the plants that horses and ponies should not eat.

NO stirrups!
The ancient Greeks rode horses, but they didn't have stirrups to put their feet into. This meant that they often fell off!

Acorns

Ragwort

Foxglove

Laburnum

Do horses drink a lot of water?

Yes – horses should always have a water supply. They need plenty of water to help wash down their food, otherwise they can get stomach pain called colic. However, some horses don't like water, especially if it's too cold.

where are horses kept?

Horses are kept in special buildings called stables. Each horse has its own room or stall, with straw or sawdust on the floor. The stalls have to be cleaned, or 'mucked out', every day to remove the horse's manure (droppings).

Owner 'mucking out'

Mother and foal

Straw

Carrots

Do cowboys ride horses?

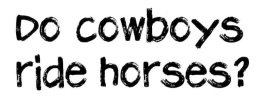

Yes – cowboys traditionally rode on horseback to move cows around their ranches (large American farms). Many cowboys still ride horses, but they also ride bulls at rodeos.

Friends or enemies?

Cowboys and 'Indians' (Native Americans) were often shown fighting in old films. In real life, this rarely happened.

What is a rodeo?

A rodeo is a show or contest where cowboys and cowgirls display their skills. These include riding wild horses, rounding up cows or using a lasso (loop of rope) Rodeos are popular in the United States, South America and Australia.

Discover

Look in books or on the Internet to find out what clothes cowboys wear.

Lasso

Cowboy

Cow

can horses dance?

Some horses can be trained to perform special ballet-like movements known as dressage. The moves include skipping, prancing, dancing sideways, balancing in difficult positions, hopping on their back legs and leaping high into the air. Austria's Lipizzaner horses are famous for their amazing dressage shows.

Lipizzaner horse

What is the smallest horse?

The Falabella miniature horse is the smallest. It is around 8 hands (80 centimetres) tall — as small as some breeds of dog! They are friendly and clever, but too small for most people to ride.

Falabella

Dance

What are your best dance moves? Try leaping high into the air like a Lipizzaner horse.

Do horses fight each other?

Yes, in the wild. A herd of wild horses has just one adult male, called a stallion. When one stallion challenges another, they rear up and fight with their front hooves.

Mini riders!

Jockeys who ride racehorses have to be as small and light as possible to make racing easier for the horse.

Quiz time

Do you remember what you have read about horses and ponies? Here are some questions to test your memory. The pictures will help you. If you get stuck, read the pages again.

3. Which horse was as small as a sheep?

page 13

4. Which horses live in swamps?

page 14

1. Which horses worked on farms?

page 5

5. What is a hotblood?

page 16

2. How can you tell a horse's age?

page 9

6. Do horses need grooming?

page 17

page 27

7. what are saddles for?

page 19

11. Do cowboys ride horses?

page 29

8. Did horses go to war?

page 21

12. what is the smallest horse?

13. Do horses fight each other?

page 29

9. why are Shetland ponies so tough?

page 23

10. Do horses drink a lot of water?

page 25

Answers

1. Shire horses
2. Experts can tell a horse's age by looking at its teeth
3. A prehistoric, sheep-sized horse called *Mesohippus*
4. Camargue horses
5. A type of horse that is fast, slender and often used in racing
6. Yes, to keep them clean and healthy
7. A saddle is a leather seat placed on a horse's back to keep its rider safe and comfortable
8. Yes, horses have been ridden into war since ancient times
9. Because the weather on the Shetland Islands, where they live, is often very cold and windy
10. Yes
11. Yes – cowboys traditionally ride horses
12. The Falabella miniature horse
13. Yes, some wild horses do

index